VERSE DIVERSIFIED #2

WITH STUFF TOO GOOD TO LOSE

James W. Faucette

Trafford rev. 05/10/2012

 www.trafford.com

North America & international
toll-free: 1 888 232 4444 (USA & Canada)
phone: 250 383 6864 ♦ fax: 812 355 4082

CONTENTS

Sonnet For John Newton

I've seen a poem lovely as a tree
In fact it's even lovelier to me
Proclaimed by sinners who have been set free
"Amazing Grace will never cease to be
With due respect to nature and to trees
One who has been redeemed with me agrees
A lovely tree will die and fade away
But God's amazing grace is here to stay.
On the sea of life John Newton was lost
And like his ship his soul was tempest tossed
Then the Holy Spirit took nature's place
Inspiring him to write, "Amazing Grace"
This song of his Soul will always be heard
Along with the Psalms and God's Holy Word.

THE BEAUTIFUL SNOW

The Omaha Publican gives the following history of this peoduction, which The London Spectator has pronounced the finest poem ever written in America. During the early part of the war of 1861, one dark Saturday night in mid winter, there died in the the Commercial Hospital in Cinncinati, a young woman over whose head only twenty and two summers had past. She had once been possessed of an enviable share of beauty, and had been, as she herself said flattered and sought for the charms of her face., but alas!, she had fallen. Among her personal effects was found the manuscript "The Beautiful Snow, which was carried immediately to Enos B. Reed a gentleman of culture and literary taste. who was at that time, Editor of the National Union. In the columns of that paper on the day following the girl's death, the poem appeared in print for the first time.When the paper containing the poem came out on Sunday morning, the body of the victim had not yet received burial. The attention of Thomas Buchanan Reed, one of the first American poets, was so taken with the stirring pathos of the verse that he followed the body to its final resting place. Such are the facts concerning her whose, "Beautiful Snow" will long be remembered as one of the brightest gems in American literature,

Misc.

A candidaate for office driving out through the country
stopped his car and yelled at a fellow plowing
in a field, "Say, I hear you've been telling folks
I'm no good for anything."
"Nope, said the fellow, "I don't know
how they found it out."

Where the puddle is shallow the weak fish stay
To drift along with the current's flow
To take the tide as it moves each day
With the idle ripples that come and go.

Grantland Rice

When the one Great scorer comes
To write against my name
It matters not that I won or lost
But how I played the game.

Grantland Rice

Epitaphs

Hello there, passing by,
As you are now, so once was I
As I am now you soon will be
Prepare yourself to follow me!
Underneath some wag wrote,
"To follow you I'm not content
Until I know which way you went!"

Here lies the body of Solomon Pease
Under the daisies, under the trees
But Pease is not here, only the pod
Pease shelled out and went home to GOD!

Epitaph to a Dog

Near this spot are deposited the remains of one
who possessed beauty without vanity, strength without
insolence, courage without ferocity, and all the virtues
of man without his devices,
This praise which would be unmeaning flattery
if inscribed over human ashes is but a just tribute
to the memory of Boatswain, a dog.

George Noel Gordon

TROUBLE FREE

Build for yourself a strong box

Fashion each part with care

When it's as strong as your hand can make it

Put all of your troubled there

Write there all thoughts of your failures

And each bitter cup that you quaff

Lock all of your heartaches in it

Then sit on the lid and laugh!!

Quotations

Flo was fond of Ebenezer

Ebb for short she called her beau

Talk of tides of love, Great Caesar!

You should have seen them,

Ebb and Flo!

anon

He drew a circle and left me out

A heretic, a rebel, a thing to flout

But love and I with the wit to win

We drew a circle and took him in!!

anon

MORE
MISCELLANEOUS

I love to watch the rooster crow
He's like so many men I know
Who brag and bluster, rant and shout
And beat their manly breasts, without
Anything at all to crow about!

John Kendrick Bangs

The Sunday school teacher told the children
to draw a picture illustrating a Biblical text,
One little girl returned with a drawing of an
airplane, with a man, woman, baby, and a pilot.
"What's this?" asked the teacher.
"The flight into Egypt", replied the little girl.
"That's Mary, Joseph, the infant Jesus,
And Pontius, the pilot."

unknown author

Tar Heel Pot Holes

It's a crying shame that I get the blame

When the fault lies not with me

When I go for a ride with my wife at my side

And a pot hole I don't see.

When we hit the bump, she gives a big jump

Then jumps all over me!

I would like to say in a friendly way

That I love this old North State,

But I would love her more

If I could be sure

Of a pot hole filling date!

Miscellaneous

George at College was running out of ideas for getting money
out of his father. Nothing he had tried lately seemed to work
He reasoned that a tricky, coy letter may appeal to the old man's
sense of humor and make him soften up. So he sat down at his
typewriter and wrote.

"Dear Dad

Gue$$ what I need mo$t of all? That$ right, Plea$e $end it along $oon,
Be$t wi$he$ and lot$ of love." Your hopeful $on, George.
The father wrote back, NOw that was a tricky letter you wrote.
I've seen NOthing exactly like it since I went to college.
NOne of us here would have thought to use the $ sign instead of an 's.'
Write us aNOther letter soon.
NOw I must close!

Uncle Mat

Four things a man must learn to do
if he would make his record true:
To think without confusion clear
To love his fellow men sincerely:
To act from honest motives purely:
To trust in God and Heaven securely.

Henry Van Dyke

THRASONICAL
BOMBAST

In promulgating your esoteric cogitations,or articulating
Your superficial sentimentalities and amicable philisophies
or psychological observations, beware of platitudinous
ponderosity,
et your conversational communicatuons possess a clarified
conciseness, a compact comprehensiveness, coalescent
Consistency and concatenated cogency. Eschew all conglomerations
Of flatulent gerrulity,jejune babblement, and asinine effectations.
Let your extemporaneous descantings and unpremeditated
Expetiations have intelligibility and voracious vivacity with-
out redomontade or thrasonical bombast. Sedulously avoid all
ploysylabic profundity, pompous prolixfity pittacaceous vacuity,
ventriloquial verbosity and vaniloquent vapidity. Shun double
extendres, prurient jocosity,and pestiforous profanity, obscurant
or apparent,

AUTHOR UNKNOWN

TRUTHFUL FANTASY

Iran to Iraq going through Kuwait

Several Arabs opened up the gate

Where Saddam Hussein met us on the street

He was shaved and clean, appearing quite neat.

He said he was innocent of doing wrong

And that President George Bush was a ding-dong

I told him then & there what any G.I. would tell

In a very short while he's going to ring your bell!!

D-Day

Perhaps of all the battles fought

The one that was most dearly bought,

Was D-DAY

And I was safe some miles away

We loaded bombers twice that day

In the costliest known affray

The U.S.A. has ever faced.

But now to me it seems a dream

The perfect planning of a team

Of dedicated men who God embraced

Who were so strategically placed

To turn the tide of World War II,

The hour came for the attack

Each soldier knew no turning back

And 5600 were doomed to die

Our freedom today is the reason why!!

THE CHURCH

There' a place overflowing with love

Where the soul sick may freely go in

A place ourchased by our God above

To give new life to those lost in sin.

When there is no other place to go

And you are oppressed without and within

Seek this place, open to high and low

Then new strength, new life will soon begin

If a burden supresses you

And your load is heavy to bear

You will find this place blesses you

And removes all of your worldly care!

Spiritual Insight

Does the blind ask his friend if he is black or white?
Can he truly discern if it is day or night?
He reads in the dark without any light
Because he walks by Faith and not by sight,
Perception is keen with his mind at peace
With loss of sight other senses increase.
Instinctively aware of a higher power
Unable to see he smells the flower
He can also hear and can feel the rain
And touch and grope with his white tipped cane
But he misses the natural beauty of earth
The budding of trees and Springtime;s new birth
God's mercy prevails along life's way
Whether or not we see when we kneel to pray!

In Concert

You are the music, I need no song

The melody you bring to me

Will last my whole life long.

Your rhytmic way concerts my day

Our lives can be one roundelay

In you there is no wrong.

If you'd but add me to your beat

I,too, would sing without a note

Our Orchestra would be complete

A sonata sweet, that no one wrote!!

RECIPE FOR HAPPINESS

Don't get (preheated)

Take (flours) to your wife

(Salt) away some(dough)

Don't (stir) up trouble

(Spice) up your life

Help those in (knead)

Don't neglect the small (fry)

(Mix) with the right crowd

Be an (Eggceptional) person

Be a sheep in the (fold)

(Blend) these ingredients

(Serve) with gladness

(Double) this recipe for best results

Filling
Station #2

When your car is running low on gas
You stop at the first station you pass
No one at all will doubt it
Your car will not run without it.

When your spirit is low
There is a place to go,
To lift up your drooping soul
A church will fill that role.

To keep yourself going
And your tank overflowing
When you feel downcast and low
A nearby Church is the place to go!

A Soul
Poetic

A soul poetic long asleep
Awoke from out the barren deep
And entered in this weary heart of mine
When I had almost given up
Refreshing spirit filled my cup
And overflowed like vintage wine.
In days gone by I felt bereft
As if God had left
My burdened soul to fade and die.
As if my God did not know
The sinful path that I did go
Before God's Son removed His wrath
And then, as cleansing from a bath
Restored my life with love divine.
And then I took my pen in hand
Wrote words I did not understand
Rhyme and verse came easy and free
I take no credit for this gift
The race may not be to the swift
But destined by the Powers that be!

The Filling
Station #1

Although our Church has empty pews
Still our preacher btings the news
To us attending to replenish
Our spirits which at times diminish.

Whenever the gospel is heard
Our feeble souls are lifted up
And as we listen to the Word
Each has an over flowing cup.

So if your tank is running low
Church is the place for you to go
And if you feel low and forlorn
Attend a Church next Sunday morn!

PLEASE
FIND ME

You see before you flesh and bone

And you are sure that it is me

It is not me, it is a clone

And where I am is mystery.

I know for sure that I'm not me

When I was born a mat of hair

Stretched from my waist down to my knee

And now I find it is not there.

Except for that I'm about the same

The cloners almost fooled me, too,

And I'm still using my same name

But where i am, I have no clue!

CALLING

Some men are called by the grace of God

To preach the Holy word

While others are called to build the pews

To seat the folks to hear the good news

Others are called to fill the space

So the Men of God may be heard.

It could be a church with a spire

With a preacher who is on fire

On a sabbath day in the spring

When the earth comes alive

And all Chrstians thrive

To celebrate Easter morn

When our Savior was reborn.

From Unknown Authors

1—If wisdom's ways you wisely seek
    Five things observe with care
    Of whom you speak, to whom you speak
    And how, and when, and where!

2—The centipede was happy quite
    Until a toad, in fun,
    Said, "Say, Which leg goes after which?"
    That stirred her up to such a pitch
    She lay distracted in a ditch
    Considering how to run!

3—Tree Nuts or Lost Souls

On the outskirts of town there was a big pecan tree by the cemetery fence. One day two boys filled up a bucket of nuts and sat down by the tree out of sight, and began dividing the nuts.

"One for you, one for me, one for you one for me, said one boy."

Several were dropped and rolled down by the fence, Another boy came riding along the road on his bicycle. As he rode by he heard voices coming from inside the cemetery. He slowed down and came back to investigate, Sure enough, he heard, "One for you, one for me, one for you, one for me."

He knew what it was. "Oh, my he shuddered, It's satan and the Lord dividing the souls."

He jumped on his bike and rode off. Around the bend he met an old man with a cane hobbling along. "Come here, quick," said the boy,

"You won;t believe what I heard. Satan and the Lord are down at the cemetery dividing up the souls." The man sais," Beat it kid, can't you see it's hard for me to walk? When the boy insisted, the old man hobbled to the cemetery." Standing by the fence they heard, "One for you, one for me, one for you, one for me." The old man whispered, "Boy, you've been telling the truth, let's see if we can see the devil himself." Shaking with fear they peered thriugh the fence but were unable to see anything. Then they heard, one for you, one for me, Now let's get those nuts by the fence. They say the lamed ols man made it back to town 5 minutes before the boy on his bike!

FOR THE YOUNG

Seek your pleasure in wholesome things

And let the foolish go their ways

Then your companions will be kings

And the reward your wisdom brings

Will make you glad through out your days.

Set yout goals while you are young

And plan with care the way you'll go

Life's a song that's to be sung

And there'll be happiness among

Those who reap where wise ones sow.

The Beautiful Snow

Oh, the snow, the beautiful snow !
Filling the sky and the earth below;
Over the housetops, over the street.
Over the heads of the people you meet.
Dancing, flirting, skipping along,
Beautiful snow, it can do no wrong.
Flying to kiss a fair ladie's cheek,
Clinging to lips in a frolicsome freak,
Beautiful snow from heaven above
Pure as an angel, gentle as love.

Oh! the snow, the beautiful snow
How the flakes gather and laugh as they go
Whirling about in their maddening fun
It plays in its glee with everyone.
Chasing, laughing, hurrying by
It lights on the face and it sparkles the eye.
And playful dogs with a bark and a bound,
Snap at the crystals as they eddy around.
The town is alive and its heart's in a glow
To welcome the coming of the beautiful snow.

How wildly the crowd goes swaying along
Hailing each other with humor and song
How the glad sleds like meteors flash by
Bright for the moment, then lost to the eye.
Ringing, swinging, dashing they go
Over the crust of the beautiful snow.
Snow so pure when it falls from the sky
As to make one regret as they see it lie
To be trampled and tracked by the thousand feet
Till it blends with the filth in the horrible street.

Once I was as pure as the snow, but I fell,
Fell like the snowflakes from heaven to hell,
Fell to be trampled as filth in the street,
Fell to be scoffed at, spit on and beat.
Pleading, cursing,dreading to die
Selling my soul to whoever would buy.
Dealing in shame for a morsel of bread.
Hating the living and fearing the dead.
Merciful God, have I fallen so low?
And yet, I was once like the beautiful snow.

Once I was fair as the beautiful snow
With an eye like its crystal and heart like its glow
Once I was loved for my innocent grace
Flattered and sought for the charms of the face
Father, mother, sister, all. God, and
Myself have I lost by my fall
The veriest wretch that goes shivering by
Will make a wide sweep when I wander too nigh.
For all that is in or above me I know
There's nothing so pure as the beautiful snow.

How strange it should be that the beautiful snow
Should fall on a sinner with nowhere to go
How strange it should be when night comes again
If the snow and the ice struck my desperate brain
Fainting, freezing, dying alone
Too wicked for prayer, too weak for a moan
To be heard in the streets of the crazy town
Gone mad in the joy of the snow coming down
To be, and to die in my terrible woe
With a bed and a shroud of the beautiful snow.

Helpless and foul as the beautifulm snow
Sinner, despair not, Christ stoopeth low
To rescue the soul that is lost in sin
And raise it to life and enjoyment again
Groaning, bleeding, dying for thee
The crucified hung on the accursed tree
His accent of mercy falls soft on thine ear
Is there mercy for me? will He heed my prayer?
O God, in the stream that for sinners did flow,
Wash me and I shall be whiter than snow.

The Primitive Baptist 1929

FICKLE
FATE

I was born on the masculine side

I knew I could never be a bride

But my sister could

She could walk down the aisle in white

On the arm of an escort full of fright

And we knew she would

She was as pretty as a doll on Chritmas morn

As cuddly as a Mother's very first born

And we all knew that

Some thought she'd wed a rich adonis

One of those guys loaded with moneys

But she chose old Pat

Pat was a fellow twice her age

Looked like a monkey just out of a cage

He worked like a horse for a meager wage

Well, Life's like that

TITLE
UNKNOWN

I walked a, ile with pleasure

She chattered all the way

But left me none the wiser

For all she had to say.

I walked a mile with sorrow

Ans ne'er a word said she

But, oh, the things I learned from her

When sorrow walked with me!

Robert Browning Hamilton

The Holy Book

Ah! The Beauty And The Glory
Of The World's Immortal Story
Of The Wisdom And The Truth
Of The Noble And Uncouth
Written For The Good Of Man
Through The Years It Did Withstand
Satan's Filthy, Fiery Hand.
To Continue Evermore
Things Which Have Gone On Before
Of What Is Now What's To Be
And What God Did To Set Man Free.
The Word Is Strength And Life To Those
Who From The World's Great Reading Chose
To Read And Seek Eternal Life,
To Overcome The Worldly Strife,
To Seek Respite From All Fear And Woe
To Hope, To Believe, And Then To Know.
Blessed Are Those Who From Its Pages
Reaped The Wisdom Of The Sages,
Ordained Before Their Lives Began
To Bring The Gospel Truth To Man.

OLD SOL

The sun has but one eye

Which brightens up the sky

Each time it passes by.

That one eye never closes

Old Soll never dozes

And darkness it disposes

EVERYWHER!!

AFTER
DINNER
SPEAKER

Begin with a touch of levity

Then add a little smile

And with a bit of brevity

The speech you make

Will take the cake

And roll 'em in the aisle!

BAN THE
HAND GUNS

The pilgrims in the early years
Arriving in a land unknown
Had reason to be filled with fears
Without protection and all alone.
Brave, though scared, they faced the chore
Of building homes, their greatest need
Then fields were plowed and at the shore
Fresh were added to their feed.
Wild beasts and red men posed a threat
To their safety and their crops
And with great courage these were met.
Arms were very much in need
They had no sheriffs nor any cops.
Today there is no such need for guns
And the use of them is much abused
Perhaps we should ban the ones
Except for rifles which are used
For hunting, Not like hand guns used today
To unecessarily maim and slay.
Today we have much protection
Army, Air Force, Navy, and Marines
Local police, sheriffs, radar detection
Watch dogs, alarms, and other means
Yet our crimes do not decrease.
This is an earnest, fervent plea
Coming from others and from me,
We would not be like the huns
So, Please, BAN HAND GUNS!!!

THE BRIDGE OF LOVE

An old man traveling a lone highway
Came at the evening which was cold and gray
To a chasm deep and wide
The old man crossed in the twilight dim.
The swollen stream held no fear for him
But he turned when safe on the other side
And built a bridge to span the tide.
"Old man," said a fellow pilgrim near
"You are wasting your strength building here,
Your journey will end with the closing day,
You never again will pass this way
You've crossed the chasm deep and wide
Why build you the bridge at eventide?"

The builder iifted his old gray head
"Good friend, in the path I've come," he said
There follows after me today
A youth whose feet must pass this way.
That chasm which was as naught to me
To that fair youth may a pitfall be
He, too, must cross in the twilight dim
Good friend, I'm building this bridge for him,"

Author Unknown

Life and Death

Between life and death there is a small thread
We call it God's spirit and Christ has said
It separates the living from the dead!

Christ died on the cross, there suffered and bled
In place of my death, He died there instead
Between life and death there is a small thread.

Spirit is more vital than daily bread
It lives in God's Word where it can be read
It separates the living from the dead

The world has always needed to be led
So the blood of Jesus had to be shed
Between life and death there is a small thread.

Give thought to the future, live without dread
Study about Jesus and the God Head.
It separates the living from the dead.

On the cross Jesus cried, to God He pled
Let them come unto me, they all will be fed
Between life and death there is a small thread
Which separates the living from the dead.

Form of Villanelle

THE HOLY BOOK

Ah! the beauty and the glory

Of the world's immortal story

Of the wisdom and the truth

Of the noble and uncouth

Written for the good of man

Through the years it did withstand

Satan's filthy fiery hand!

To continue evermore

Things which have gone on before

And what is now, and what's to be

And what God did to set man free

The Word is strength and life to those

Who from the world's great reading chose

To read and seek eternal life

To overcome the worldly strife

To seek respite from all fear and woe

To hope, to believe, and then to know

ASTRONAUTS

Beyond the beautiful blue skies
Invisible to human eyes
Are many, many nations
Sojourns into space are planned
So astronauts from our great land
Can go there on vacation!!

Prisoner's Lament

Within these dark prison walls

There is much time to reflect

The farther a person falls

The more there is to correct.

Somewhere along life's way

I gave in to temptation

And was quickly led astray

Not a bit of hesitation

Now within this wall of flesh

My soul is like this walls

There is no hope to escape

I'm here until death calls

And all I do is sit and gape

At these gray prison walls!!

WEATHERMAN

The weatherman had doppler

But he didn't know

Which way the wind would blow

He predicted rain

But once again

The ground is covered with snow!

A FARMER'S
DAYVORCE

A farmer walked into an attorney's office wanting to file for a divorce. The attorney asked, "May I help you?" The farmer said, "Yea, I want to get one of those dayvorces." The attorney asked, "Well, do you have any grounds?" The farmer said," Yea, I got about 140 acres," The attorney said, "No, you don't understand, do you have a case?" The farmer said, "No, I aint got a Case, but i've got a John Deere." The attorney said, No. you still don't understand, have you got a grudge?"

The farmer said, "Yea I got a grudge, that' where I park my John Deere." The attorney said, No Sir, I mean do you have a suit?" The farmer said, "Of course, I wear it to Church on Sundays."

The attorney said, well sir, does your wife beat you up or anthing?' The farmer said, "No. we both get up about 4:30." The attorney then said, "Well is she a nagger or anything of that sort?" The farmer said, "No, she's a little white gal, but our last child was a nagger, an that's why I want this here dayvorce!"

Tribute To The Disabled G.I.

*The price of freedom is high, it is bought
with the lives of the young, blood, sweat, and tears.
The disabled for life, a terrible thought!!
The cost of freedom should always be taught
to children in school, in their young years
That their freedom is high, it has been bought,
with sticks and stones and lances and spears
Disabling many with hardly a thought.
Benefits of fredom may come to naught
if we who are free when the need appears
forget that our freedom by blood was bought.
Hospital and rest homes\ nurses are fraught
with the lame and the maimed so full of fears
of being disabled, a grievous thought.
Let us all who are whole never be caught
without true allegiance so he who hears
knows that the cause of freedom is bought
By the disabled and dead . . . what a thought!!*

Tribute To The Disabled G.I.

The price of freedom is high, it is bought
with the lives of the young, blood, sweat, and tears.
The disabled for life, a terrible thought!!
The cost of freedom should always be taught
to children in school, in their young years
That their freedom is high, it has been bought,
with sticks and stones and lances and spears
Disabling many with hardly a thought.
Benefits of fredom may come to naught
if we who are free when the need appears
forget that our freedom by blood was bought.
Hospitals and rest homes are over wrought
With the lame who are fikked with fears
of being disabled, a grievous thought!
Let us all who are free never be caught
without true allegiance that any who hears
knows the cause of freedom is bought
By the dead and disabled,. What a thought!!

NO IDLE MINDS

The devil's workshop is an idle mind
He also delights in the unemployed
Think and work and eave the devil behind!

The Bible says to seek and youm will find
There's always more than one way to avoid
The devil's workshop and an idle mind.

Get up and go, help the lame and the blind
A small effort will leave you over joyed
And you'll leave old beelzebub behind.

Find ways to deviate from daily grind
Think positive, you wont need Sigmund Freud
Forsake the devil and make up your mind.

Not everyone you meet is good and kind
And idle thoughts make some folks paranoid
But positive thoughts leave old satan behind.

Control negatives to which you're inclined
Some of them may cause you to be annoyed
The devil's workshop is an idle mind
But positive thoughts leave satan behind.

AVE MARIA

When the angel did appear

And whispered, "have no fear"

It calmed the troubled breast of Maria.

The one our God has blessed

Somewhere above the rest

She is the very best, Maria!

The one Our God chose to be

The mother of the one to set his people free.

He blessed Maria, caressed Maria,

She is of sweet accord

The mother of our Lord

Her name will always be adored

Ave Maria—Ave Maria!!

OLD
MAC DOUGAL

Old MacDougal had a bugle
Blew it every day
While Old MacDonald on his farm
Pitched a lotta hay
MacDougal was a music man,
He made the people sing
That's how MacDougal got the name
Of Mac the Bugle king

MacDonald said to his wife one day
I'm getting tired of pitching hay
Old MacDougal knows the way
I'll buy myself a horn

Well, he learned to play
Like Harry James
Surrounded himself with pretty dames
Went out to Vegas to play the games
Just as sure as he was born.

Now MacDonald's back down on a farm
Where the Roulette wheels can do him no harm
He's up each morning at the break of day
Back out there pitchuing hay!!!

I AM

I was regretting the past
and fearing the future
Suddenly, my Lord was speaking.
"My name is I Am"
He paused,I waited, He continued.
"When you live in the past
With its mistakes and regrets
it's hard. I am not there,
for my name is not I WAS.
When you live in the future
with its problems and fears,
It is hard.
I am not there for my name is
Not I WILL BE
When you live in the moment
It is not hard.
I am here, for my name is I AM,"

AUTHOR UNKNOWN

and idle thoughys make some folks paranoid
But active minds leave old Satan behind

Cnntrol negatives to which you're inclined
Some of which may cause you to be annoyed
The devils workshop is an idle mind
But if you try you'll leave him far behind!!

BELLS OF
CHRISTMAS

Christmas time is near
Time for joyful song
The best time of year
When bells go ding dong
Boys, girls, old folks .too
Love to hear the bells
I do too, don't you
Love the Christmas bells?
Some bells ting-a-ling
Others go ding-dong
Come now let's all sing
Sing this happy song

Christmas bells ringing
And girls and boys singing
Bring us Christmas cheer
The spirit of love
Sent down from above
Makes this the merriest,
Happiest, Very best, time of the year
Tinga-linga-ling, tinga-linga-ling
Tinga-linga-ling-ding dong!!!

Acrostic for
Ruth F. Allen

Remembrance is a precious gift

Useful to keep he spirit young

The Thoughts of childhood brings a lift

Helping us to recall the young days among

Family and friends we shared life with.

After recalling days gone by

Like a book, we turn the page

Leaving us with a breathless sigh

Even though we know that as we age

Nothing can change the days gone by!!

NEIGHBORHOOD

I walked through the old neighborhood
and fond memories returned to me
None were bad, they all were good
The days of youth when I was carefree.

The only things to spoil my day
were the run down homes, once so neat
and the weeded fields where we would play
Instead of playing in the street.

Our neighborhood was filled with pride
The lawns were mowed and always green
The houses painted, trimmed outside
Signs of decay were seldom seen.

The tenants now seem not to care
they must be s a different breed
Trash and debris are everywhere
Our neighborhood has gone to seed!!

Spring Revival

Welcome sun, disperse the clouds—shine!

Welcome wind, dry out the land—blow!

And gentle breeze, come stir the trees

That now lie covered with snow.

Welcome Spring, you bring a new year

And new life to the dormant trees

Which winter robbed of their cheer.

Shine golden rays to warm the earth

And bring forth buds of daffodil

Filling us with carefree mirth

When warmth replaces winter's chill!

TODAY'S
SOUP

I'm not too sure about the soup du jour

It is not clear which day it may be

I'd feel better when dining

With better defining

Such as soup de d'au jour'dhui***

*** soup of today

DECEPTION

A large invasion has just taken place
Although our citizens are unaware
We have been invaded from outer space.

These aliens look like us in the face
And you can see them almost anywhere
A large invasion fas just taken place

They resemble the white or the black race
Their knack for changing image is quite rare
We have been invaded from outer space!

These aliens are endowed with much grace
Their mein and manner are so debonair
A surprising invasion just took place

Smart, wise, and competent in every case
They are so adept, thay have savoir-faire
Few know we have been invaded from space.

We are holding a deuce, they hold an ace
Whatever they do, they do with a flair
A dreaded invasion has taken place
We have been invaded from outer space!!

Walk the Aisle

The well worn path
Where feet have trod
To allay the wrath
Of our God
Where today's saints
Purged from their sin
Eased from their plaints
Have entered in
To fellowship
With others who
Have shed the grip
OF SUPRESSION

This is the aisle of any Church
Where man or child
Can end the search
For peace within.
You, too,may take
This step, begin-
Ths past forsake
And end Depression

THE UNSEEN HAND

We accept the miracles of today
Spaceships, computers, and color TV
So many miracles have come our way.

We see the combines bundle up the hay
Electric fences closing in the lea.
We expect the miracles of today.

We must admit we miss the horse's neigh
Since tractors plow where horses used to be
Work easing miracles have come our way.

Whoever we may be we have to say
We are blessed by many things we cannot see
Unexpected miracles come our way.

The greatest miracle brought us a ray
Of hope and truth—an answer to our plea
The miracle of Christ has come our way.

Clouds have passed, skies are no longer gray
Life is now easier for you and me
Because of the miracles of today.
So many miracles have come our way!!!

Aging Rudolph

Rudolph works one night a year
Guiding the other eight reindeer
He'll soon let Prancer lead the pack
So he can rest his aching back.

Pulling the sleigh from shore to shore
Makes Rudolph's back mighty sore
He thinks next year he may retire
And sit home warmly by the fire.

Now Santa's sleigh zips through the air
Snow flakes flying everywhere
Wait for him and he'll be there
To leave you gifts, so don't despair.

Just sit around, don't watch the clock
Did you forget to hang your sock?
This is the best night of the year
The night Christ in the flesh was here!

SANTA'S COMING

Santa's coming through the air
Snowflakes flying everywhere
Pretty soon he will be there
with lots of toys and gifts to share.
Of all the reindeer, Santa chose
Rudolph with his shiny nose
To guide his sleigh through heavy snows
and the ice cold winter wind that blows.
Yes, Santa's coming through the snow
Rudolph's nose is all aglow
Before you hear his HO! HO! HO!
Put out cookies and Cocoa.
And this is just to let you know
His favorite cookie is OREO!!

LOVE

Love has always been
Love will always be
Not only my love for you
Not also your love for me.

Love moves very deep
Love seeks not its own
Love is a promise to keep
Love is never alone.

Love is like a ricochet
You'll find this to be true
The more love you give away
The more comes back to you!

NO REST
FOR THE SUN

Morning, noon and night
The sun is shining bright
Somewhere>
When we are in bed at night
The sun is bringing light-
Over There.
When we are in bed at rest
The light has left the west
ts warmth and life to share.
Though our sun stands still
and fixed in outer space
In time appointed it will
shine upon some other place.
Our earth spins on its axis
sharing our wonderful sun
which remains steady, the fact is
Our Earth is on the run!!

BALDERDASH

The sun is shining bright tonight

The rain is pouring down

Not a drop of water is in sight

The green leaves on the trees are brown

The dog meowed and the cat barked

Birds filled the trees and sang

We sat outside beside the hearth

And answered the phone before it rang.

This may seem a bit weird to you

And that is what it is meant to be

A little foolishness now anmd then

May turn a frown into a grin!!

Embraced by the Free

The borders of our land are open wide
To admit those who would be truly free
Adjust to our ways for which many died.

If you have been lucky to get inside
our great country,be good and live that we
may keep entry to our land opened wide

Realize that in order to abide
with us, you must obey our laws and be
content in our ways for which many died.

You need not fawn,make sure you have tried
to learn our language—be grateful so that we
may keep entry to our land opened wide.

As a citizen we hope you take pride
to belong, to accept, and to agree
to uphold this land for which many died.

Write home to your folks, let them know you side
with the U.S.A.—that will be the key
to keep entry to our land opened wide.
Conform to our way, for which many died!!

Where Night
Meets Day

Transcendental meditation

Ever present, ever deep

Occupies my waking thoughts

Penetrates my deepest sleep

Mysterious insight,revelation

Channels once unknown, unsought

Certify realization

Show what mind of man has brought

Such profound deliberation

Tends to reveal the depth of height

Aided by man's concentration

Accelerates the end of night!

NO REST
FOR THE SUN

The sun has but one eye

Which brightens the sky

Each time it passes by.

Away up in the air

The eye never closes

The sun never dozes

And darkness it disposes

EVERYWHERE!

CHAIN
REACTION

A dozen doves were feeding there
Observed by a feline stranger
Not one of the doves seemed aware
Of the impending danger.
Neither was the cat aware
Two eyes had him in view
A mongrel dog approaching there
Was only passing through.
The dog tore after the cat
Causing the doves to flee
To a natural habitat
The safety of a nearby tree.
Speaking of the cat,
Whatever happened to him?
Just below the doves
Sat the cat safe on a limb!

Farmer's
Reward

The new ground was sown in field corn and wheat
to lay in store for the cold winter time
when the bare fields afford little to eat.

Hard work and weeding kept the corn field neat
It helped to strew fertilizer and lime
When the new ground budded with corn and wheat.

After plowing all day he came home beat
He relied on his know-how and the clime
to make the bare fields offer more to eat.

The sun came down with unrelenting heat
But he was a young man and in his prime
His land abounded with field corn and wheat.

The daily grind was now almost complete
He had survived briers, insects, amd grime
The ground now flourished with plenty to eat.

When he reaped just before hoarfrost and rime
His feeling was rapture, he felt sublime
When the ground was cleared of field corn and wheat
His larder was filled with plenty to eat!!

Villanelle form

DRIVEN
TO DRINK

For sixty days no rain came down
Rivers and lakes were almost dry
The once green grass had turned to brown.

Water supply alarmed the town
The living plants began to die
Thirsty for rain which did not come down.

Tempers on edge, smile turned to frown
Everyone knew the reason why
Because all of the green had turned to brown.

Those with gardens wished they could drown
Their crops which now began to fry
It had been so long since rain came down.

No one felt like playing the clown
All were praying to God on high
To restore the grass now a deep brown.

The local pub," The Town & Gown"
Eased the woes of many a guy
For sixty days no rain came down
The once green grass still was brown.

Style of Villanelle

SPECIAL
OLYMPICS

There was a time some years ago

When crippled kids were full of woe

No hope for a better day,

No jumping rope, no games to play

No help was near, there was no cure

The unshed tear, grief to endure

Today there's joy, the lame compete

Each girl and boy at olympics meet

To feel a part, they all live now

A gift of hearts, our gifts endow!

Long Stemmed Roses

I know that she likes roses

She likes the red ones best

She will recall those on the wall

Beneath the bluebird's nest

No words can speak like flowers

And she'll know what they say

They will cheer her lonely hours

And brighten up her day

I'll still send her the roses

Although we're now apart

The sweet perfume will fill her room

But the thorns will pierce my heart.

LOVE
FOREVER

There'll always be winter and spring
There will always be birds on the wing
There will always be new songs to sing
And there will always be love
There will always be a blooming flower
There will always be that shining hour
There will always be a higher power
And there will always be love
There will always be a deep blue sea
There will always be a land that's free
There will always be a you and me
Because there will always be love.

AND THERE WILL ALWAYS BE LOVE.
There will always be new songs to sing
And there'll always be love
There'll always be a blooming flower
There'll always be that shining hour
There'll always be a higher power
And there'll always be love
here'll always be a deep blue sea
There'll always be a land that's free
There'll always be a you and me
Because there will always be LOVE.

DESERT
HARDSHIP

The soldier wiped the dust from his eyes
The desert heat was more than he could bear
He looked hopefully to the skies
but found no relief from his burden there

The hot sand blistered his naked feet
No wind, no breeze, no help was near
He almost gave in to defeat
but love of life to him was dear.

Two more hours before the sun
would sink below the horizon
Then he would walk, maybe run
to a haven he once laid eyes on

When darkness came he started out
and weary though his sun baked bones
He almost broke into a shout
when he saw a sign," TELEPHONES"

He knew with joy that help was nigh
that soon he would be with his friends
Again he looked up to the sky
To thank God for the help HE sends

Stand Up and be Counted

We accept the good gifts of our land
and each and all of us should stand
behind our troops on foreign land.

He who would not change wrong to right
who lacks the courage to go and fight
perhaps is overcome with fright

United . . . the very first word
of our great country was conferred
to bind us in a common cause
and to uphold our country's laws.

To honor and respect our chief
to dispel doubt, promote belief
that he has the guts and the gall
to do what he thinks is best for all.

Within our land there are those
who would desert unto our foes
but we who have been here our lives long
will resist the negative ones among
us and will back our Chief to the hilt
to preserve this land which our forebears built!!

Happy
Birthday

Happy birthday, you're 62

Look at all you have going for you

You're over the hill the humps are behind

Now coast on down with a satisfied mind

And add to those other two things of surety

the best by far . . . SOCIAL SECURITY!!

ACROSTIC FOR PRESTON MOSES

Preserving the historic acts
Reaching back to years gone by
Entering interesting facts
So we may know where when and why.
Trusted by all of his fellow men
Of Chatham and country wide
Never to fail their trust and then

Made sure that honesty applied.
Often going the extra mile
Supplying every publishing need
Each PACKET issue well worth while
Shows that Preston is special indeed!

** Preston was publisher and Editor of "The Packet"
a historical publication of Chatam, Virginia

HEALTHY, WEALTHY & WISE

Whenever you want a cigarette,
A substitute will stand the test
Chew some gum or suck a mint
Clear your lungs, strenghthen your chest.

That's the way I beat the rap
I know it will work for you
You can escape the money trap
And feel great whenever you do!

When I smoked at 20 cents a pack
I did not realize the cost
But at today's price
A small fortune will soon be lost!

Heed this friendly advice, brother
I would not with you joke.
A word to thr wise will suffic
And your money will not go up in smoke!!!

LONGER
LIFE

You are three score and ten
So we've all been told
We both remember when
That was considered old
But it is not true today
We have come a long, long way
And our modern gage*
You've only reached middle age.

* varied spelling of guage

An Ode to the Pill

Here's to you little pill

although at times your'e hard to swallow

It is true you have cured many an ill

But you've cost us many a dollar

Toast to the Pill

Here's to you littie pill

Though at times you're hard to swallow

It's true you've cured many as ill

But you've cost us many a dollar !

THE UNSEEN CAT

You asked me," Where is the cat?"

I don't know where the cat is at

But a cat is not like a bat up there flying around

The cat is probably chasing a rat, somewhere on the ground.

I will see if I can find the cat

Unlike Seuss's cat she is not in a hat

And unlike Jack Sprat she does eat fat.

I've looked everywhere, high and low

But where the cat is, I don't know

So that is your answer . . . and that is that!!

THE HOLY BOOK

AH! THE BEAUTY AND THE GLORY
OF THE WORLD'S IMMORTAL STORY
OF THE WISDOM AND THE TRUTH
OF THE NOBLE AND UNCOUTH
WRITTEN FOR THE GOOD OF MAN
THROUGH THE YEARS IT DID WITHSTAND
SATAN'S FILTHY, FIERY HAND.
TO CONTINUE EVERMORE
THINGS WHICH HAVE GONE ON BEFORE
OF WHAT IS NOW WHAT'S TO BE
AND WHAT GOD DID TO SET MAN FREE.
THE WORD IS STRENGTH AND LIFE TO THOSE
WHO FROM THE WORLD'S GREAT READING CHOSE
TO READ AND SEEK ETERNAL LIFE,
TO OVERCOME THE WORLDLY STRIFE,
TO SEEK RESPITE FROM ALL FEAR AND WOE
TO HOPE, TO BELIEVE, AND THEN TO KNOW.
BLESSED ARE THOSE WHO FROM ITS PAGES
REAPED THE WISDOM OF THE SAGES,
ORDAINED BEFORE THEIR LIVES BEGAN
TO BRING THE GOSPEL TRUTH TO MAN.

SWANNY RIVER

Down at the river where I first met you
The grass was green and the sky was blue
Not a single cloud in the sky above
What a wonderful thing to be in love!

The birds were singing in the trees above
Everything is music when you're in love
I did not see nor hear the birds
I only heard your musical words
When you told me of the joy you shared
That you loved me too and you really cared.

Now the years have passed and we are old
The once green grass has turned to gold
Although the years have hurried by
The blue sky still reflects in your eye
We recall the coo of the mating dove
What a wonderful thing to be in love!!

STILL SMALL VOICE

The stillness of the night may speak to you
Although you may not hear its silent call
The message somehow, somewhere will get through.

True peace, serenity it will bring, too
So be alert and you will feel it fall
When the still small voice whispers unto you.

This mysterious insight will imbue
you and release you though you be a thrall
This message clean and clear will come through.

You're lucky if you're chosen from the few
for this blessing which will not come to all
but this stillness of night may speak to you.

This force from without the ethereal blue
will penetrate a thick resisting wall
bringing this vital message unto you.

Be expectant or you will miss the clue
It can come to anyone great or small
This stillness of the night may speak to you
If so, this message will surely get through!

REWARD
YOURSELF

To do yourself a world of good
and reap he best life has to give
a Church is in your beighborhood
where God's Word tells you how to live.
Just walk to Church, it is not far
the exercise will help your health,
No need for bus—no need for car
There you'll receive God's kind of wealth.

PUBLIC TV

See the world from your favorite chair

Turn on the TV you will find it there

Scenes from the past will fill your eye

With wonder galore beneath the sky

The beauty of mountains on display

Fish and animals, quite an array

And people of color from foreign lands

With works of art from their skillful hands

So get ready for a delightful treat

Turn to Public TV and take your seat!!

Power

Power measured by a horse

Power measured by a watt

Power neasured by a force

Power measured by a knot

Most of us lean on power unseen

The Spirit leads us on

By Faith we know

The best way to go

And which power to lean upon

Power sent from above

The mighty power of God's love!!

An Ode to the Pill

The pill is small, but all in all
It packs a powerful punch.
You may take one at any time
Or two or three at lunch.
Just one a day will make you strong
And keep doctor's away all year long.
How many pills are taken each day?
For aches and ills, no one can say
But rest assured, without a doubt.
Druggists will not your pills give ou!!

MOVE THE BAIT

The cock roach committee was meeting

To discuss important matters at hand

It seemed some of thr members were eating

In a place the committee had banned

The mortality rate was increasing

They were fearful of becoming extinct

When the chairman demanded the ceasing

Of eating from under the kitchen sink!!

MENIAL LABOR

Don't send everyone to college

We need some folks to do the work

Which requires such little knowledge

Educated people shirk.

Some wise man said it long ago

when burdened low with nature's griefs

And this is true as we all know

Too few indians, too many chiefs~~

KEEPING ON

An eighty year old man named Bill

Was thought to be "Over the Hill"

It surprised one and all

When his wife had the gall

To make it known," She's on the Pill"

GET RELIEF

Many poems make an impression

and some poems relieve depression

If you are depressed

I'd like to suggest

That a small bit of cash

will get you 'Ogden Nash'

Be Wise

If wisdom's ways you wisely seek

Five things observe with care

Of whom you speak

To whom you speak

And how, and when, and where!

Author Unknown

CREATION

The earth was without form and bare
When God said to Jesus His Son,
"Let us make man and put him there
to live and love and get things done."

We'll separate the land and the seas
and send a star they will call the sun
We'll send the wind for a breeze
and keep our eyes on everyone.

From the earth miracles will spring
so that man may have everything
We'll give him many things to eat
Fresh farm produce, fruit, milk, and meat

And from the seas will come rare fish
We will fulfill his every wish
He will be happy in every way
but he must worship us and pray!

CAROLINA WREN

I've never heard another bird

Sing as sweetly as the wren

Note after note from its warbling throat

Fills the air and then,

After a brief interlude iy gets in the mood

To begin all over again

The wren is a tiny bird

And no oral nor written word

Can explain its desire to sing

But when the notes pour out

There's no shadow of doubt

It's the most talented bird on the wing!!!

BIRD BRAINS

No prettier sight than geese in flight

Flying in formation

We belittle bird brains

But no one explains

This phenomenal sensation!

A Natural Symphony

God sends to us a symphony
Not in a particular key.
The wind sounds like the violin
Thunder blends the bass drums in
The lightning brings the video
And raindrops pianissimo.
The falling snow adds to the scene
With stiff icicles in between
Dripping to set a nice tempo.
At times the beat is fast—then slow.
The brds fly to escape the storm
And geese fly by in the "V" form.
Their honks supply the needed horn.
Combined a symphony is born!
Tune your ear to this interlude
And you will enjoy a tranquil mood!

PUNDITS SENT TO ME AT CHRISTMAS

by: Mary Ellen Turlington Johnston Hale
A poet of renown in N.C.

Have the season's jolly" days
Turned in to Holi-daze?

Relaxation—have you shunned it?
Why not stop and read a pundit/

Should a smiling psychic
foretell bad things
ad tedium?
Would you be forgiven
Should you strike a happy medium?

Should a prince on horseback
dismount onto the strand,
Could you say, that would make
Foot prince in the sand?

Little elves outside my house
busy all night through
polish every blade of grass
And they dew windows, too.

If the famous painter
wore a smock
with drooping sleeves and folds
around the neck
Somebody remarking on the fit
would have said,
"Your smock's too loose, Lautrec."

At a breakfast table
juices poured and ready
Everyone you'd hope would be
Seated, still, and steady
Raucous behavior
Bad manners showing ptobably
Would be enough
To get the juices flowing!

The apple fell on Newton
and in dliberation
He understood the gravity
of the situation !